SEAS...

WHAT I SEE
IN SPRING

by Danielle J. Jacks

TABLE OF CONTENTS

Words to Know. 2

What I See in Spring. 3

Let's Review!. 16

Index. 16

WORDS TO KNOW

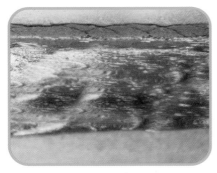
puddles

rain boots

rainbow

raincoat

sun

umbrella

WHAT I SEE IN SPRING

Spring is here!

snow

Snow melts.

Rain falls.

raincoat

I wear a raincoat.

umbrella ·····▶

I use an umbrella.

rain
boot

I wear rain boots.

puddle

I jump in puddles!

13

sun

I see the sun.

14

rainbow ·····▶

I see a rainbow!

LET'S REVIEW!

Point to the items we wear in spring.

INDEX

puddles 13

rain 7

rain boots 12

rainbow 15

raincoat 9

snow 5

sun 14

umbrella 11